Bobby
the Alien

Written by Amanda Cant

Illustrated by Julie Park

It was Monday morning.
'Hello, everybody,' said Kelly.
'I went to a party at the weekend.
We had pizza!'

'I went to see a film,' said Rosie.

'I went shopping,' said Tilak.

'I played football,' said Sam.

'I played a computer game,' said Mo.

'And I saw a spaceship!' said Bobby.
Everybody looked at him.

'It landed in my garden,' said Bobby.
'An alien got out!'

Tilak said, 'Were you scared?'
'No!' said Bobby.

'We played a computer game,'
said Bobby.
'But the alien wasn't very good.
His fingers were too long!'

'I wish I could meet an alien,'
laughed Mo.

'Then we played football,' said Bobby.
'But the alien wasn't very good.
His legs were too short!'

'I wish I could meet an alien,'
laughed Sam.

'Then we went shopping,' said Bobby.
'But everybody was scared of the alien.
They all ran away!'

'I wish I could meet an alien,' said Tilak.

'Then we watched a video,' said Bobby.
'But the alien was scared!
He ran away!'

'I wish I could meet an alien,' said Rosie.

'Then we had some pizza,' said Bobby.
'But the alien didn't like it,
so I had his too!'

'I wish I could meet an alien,' said Kelly.

'Then the alien got back in his spaceship,'
said Bobby. 'He flew away.'

'Hello, everybody,' said Mrs Hall.
'What did you do at the weekend?'

'I went to a party,' said Kelly.

'I went to see a film,' said Rosie.

'I went shopping,' said Tilak.

'I played football,' said Sam.

'I played a computer game,' said Mo.

'What about you, Bobby?' said Mrs Hall.
'Oh, I just stayed at home and watched
a video!' said Bobby.
They all laughed.